THE SCARCEST COMMODITY

Dennis Peter Barba, Jr.

IdeaBytes Publishing, Inc.

Cleveland, Ohio

IdeaBytes Publishing, Inc.
25350 Rockside Road
Cleveland, Ohio 44146
Visit our Web Site at http://www.idea-bytes.com

Printed in the United States of America
First Printing: December 2001

30 29 28 27 26 25 24 23 22 21

Library of Congress Cataloging-in-Publication Data is available

ISBN 0-9715947-0-8

Book cover design by Robert Craig
Editor David Dalton
Printing by Excel Printing & Graphics

To Monica, Peter, Owen & Andrew

Special thanks to Willie Pietersen and Michael Fenlon of the Columbia Graduate School of Business.

The idea for this book came from your lectures and from Willie's teachings on strategy and clarity of thought.

TABLE OF CONTENTS

INTRODUCTION:
The Scarcest Commodity

Economists have never been held in particularly high regard. It's risky to launch a book on a blatantly negative note, but so be it.

Part prognosticator and part historian, an economist's craft can be likened to a sort of shotgun wedding between applied statistics and social psychology. As a group, television weather forecasters may or may not be more accurate, but they have the advantage of knowing that hurricane season aside, the stakes riding on the precision of their estimates are not as high.

Still, economists have, since Thomas Malthus and Adam Smith, managed to claim a significant share of the academic high ground. If Federal Reserve Chairman Alan Greenspan is not the nation's most successful intellectual, he's certainly (for now) the most followed. And it's worth occasionally reminding your friends down the hall in accounting and marketing that each year since 1969, the good folks at the Alfred Nobel Foundation have named a laureate in economics – the only non-natural science to hold the distinction. (Interesting side note: Academic and research-types have exhibited a virtual stranglehold on the award, running the table for 31 straight years. No policy maker, including Mr. Greenspan, has been honored by the Foundation, for reasons no one seems compelled to explain.)

Economics – once called the dismal science – remains relevant because despite the biases and agendas of some practitioners, it has never strayed far from its original mission. Traditionally defined, economics is the study of how a society elects to allocate its scarce resources.

Scarcity is a relative term, of course, but it's safe to say that prior to the industrial revolution, the resources in question were commodities, or close to commodity in nature; farm products, petrol, livestock, precious metals, timber, spices, and the like.

In the information age scarcity enters in to discussions involving energy sources, skilled labor, and venture capital.

The scarcest commodity of all? Actually, the absolute scarcest commodity can be the make-or-break factor as you plan for financial success. It is something you invest in, but not in the way you're probably thinking. The scarcest commodity of all is not oil, platinum, plutonium, or vital organs needed for transplant recipients.

The scarcest commodity is *Clarity of Thought.*

I have counseled hundreds of bright, highly educated people about their personal finances. Surgeons, CEOs, trust beneficiaries and recent retirees come to me for advice, then expect a game plan after a half-hour conversation. Isn't it amazing that someone who has worked long and hard to accumulate wealth will take a haphazard approach to investing?

Or worse, many investors panic if a stock or mutual fund drops marginally in price, or is outperformed during a short period by another investment. They forget or ignore the reasons for making the investment in the first place, then try to rationalize selling out of the position.

The timid investor will say, "let's sell and get back in after the market bottoms out." The motive is simply to re-allocate the proceeds into whatever sector happens to be hot that particular week. That's usually a bad move.

CLEAR THOUGHT #1

Avoid panic selling during market pullbacks.

If the fundamentals (the reasons that convinced you to buy the stock) have not changed, and the price drop can be attributed to normal market volatility or "noise", it's probably worth staying in the position.

It's strange that when stock prices drop, many investors get nervous and sell in a panic. Ask yourself: is there any other market in the world where people sell as prices *get cheaper*? In fact, in the framework of a long-term investment strategy, dips or corrections become buying opportunities.

Ironically, the sheer volume of information available to the modern investor makes the process more complicated. The gap between the volume of information and our ability to make sense of it is expanding. Unprecedented technological developments make information instantly available to nearly anyone. Stock and bond prices from exchanges around the globe are available in real-time. Internet bulletin boards and chatrooms instantly spread rumors and predictions about corporate earnings, mergers, and management shake-ups. Hundreds of publications tout what they believe is the next Oracle or Microsoft, and at least two cable networks in North America report financial news 24 hours a day.

This information glut tempts investors to act impulsively, focusing on today, this week or this month. This leads to chasing yesterday's winning stocks and funds. But unfortunately the party's usually over, leading to disappointment when the stellar returns are not repeated.

So much for clear thinking.

CLEAR THOUGHT #2

Winning investors ignore their emotions and follow a logical, predetermined course of action.

Losers chase performance. (If you learn only that from this book, it will have succeeded.)

Trying to time the market, or waiting for the next great correction can be a dangerous game. Far too many individuals sell most of their portfolios during market declines, never to return. While they wait for the next great correction, they end up with a loss, and miss out on the next advance. Had they taken the time to execute a strategic long-term plan to begin with, they probably would have maintained their focus. That's why it's important to focus on the long term and keep emotions in check during periods of short-term volatility.

Consider the track record of junk bond king Michael Milken. His career was certainly controversial, but long before his legal troubles he was generally acknowledged as perhaps the most innovative financial mind of the twentieth century, amassing a billion dollar fortune.

Here's the point: Milken – who is cultivating a new reputation as an incredibly generous philanthropist – says he reviews his personal stock portfolio very infrequently, perhaps once every three or four years. He knows that financial markets are inherently volatile, and does not let near term drops distract him from his plan.

CLEAR THOUGHT #3

If you have at least ten years before retirement, ignore market volatility and focus on the long-term. And fair warning: as markets move higher over time, volatility will *increase*.

> *The single largest investment most Americans make in a life-time is the purchase of a home, but no one bothers to determine the current market value of their home each morning.*
>
> *Why? Because rational people buy the best house they can afford, confident that it should appreciate in value.*
>
> *They know they can't resell a house thirty days after closing and expect to make a profit that exceeds the purchase price, improvements and the real estate agent's commission.*
>
> *A house purchase is a strategic acquisition. It is bought knowing it won't be sold in thirty days or even thirty months.*
>
> *The same thinking should apply to your other investments.*

CLEAR THOUGHT #4

Concentrate on what can happen over the next five to ten years...not the next five to ten weeks.

This book will help you get your financial act together and prepare for a prosperous future.

Specific topics include:

• How to select your team of advisors.

• The importance of diversification.

• Stock selection techniques.

• Asset allocation.

• Basic insurance and estate planning strategies.

Whether you are a recent college graduate, a mid-career professional, or a successful executive thinking about retirement planning, this book will leave you with much to think about.

SOCIAL INSECURITY?

Having enough money for retirement is one of the biggest worries Americans encounter. According to the Social Security Administration, the sources of retirement income for Americans are as follows:

Public Assistance	1%
Earnings	26%
Investment Income	24%
Pension Plans	21%
Other Income	5%
Social Security Income	23%

The Federal Government estimates that more than 50% of the population over age 65 would be living in poverty without Social Security benefits. Further evidence towards poor planning for the average citizen.

With many companies moving from defined benefit plans to defined contribution plans, many future retirees will not be able to depend upon pension funds as a source of retirement earnings. If you are one of these individuals and your employer's program is dependent on your savings, it will be even more important to implement a strategic financial blueprint.

As noted in the chart above, over half of the average retiree's earnings come from either personal savings or from income generated by employment. If you are still working, are you really retired?

CHAPTER ONE:
The Pre-Planning Process

Dennis P. Barba Jr.

1. NALP (Begin with the End in Mind)

In order to be successful at investment planning, you need to ask yourself:

– Where do I *need* to be at some point in time?

– Where do I *want* to be at some point in time?

– Where am I now?

When implementing a financial plan, you need to carefully consider all three questions. You need to examine realities. You need to think of where you want or need to be, and then envision what it will take to get you there. Here is where *NALP* comes in handy. What is NALP? NALP is PLAN spelled backwards. This will help you remember an important principle of finance: begin with the end in mind.

Said a different way, you have to work backwards to start planning!

Here's a helpful definition of the word plan (spelled the right way) as defined by John Maxwell:

P redetermine a course of action

L ay out your goals

A djust your priorities

N otify key personnel

EXAMPLE:

Fred, who's 35, wants to retire at 50 with $5 million. With that established, he needs a plan that will get him there in 15 years. Defining what he wants will get him focused on the realities of his situation, and will help determine options that could lead to achieving his goals.

Fred's current situation is as follows:

Current Savings	$500,000
Annual Savings Amount	$ 25,000
Return on Savings	10%
Retirement Goal	$5,000,000
Desired Retirement Age	50 (15 Years)

Is Fred's goal easily attainable, or does he need to clarify his thoughts relative to retirement planning? Let's take a closer look:

Future value of $500,000 in 15 years at 10% return	$2,088,624
Future value of $25,000 annual savings at 10% return	$ 794,312
Total Value of savings at age 50	$2,882,936

As you can see from this quite simple calculation, it will be near impossible for Fred to accumulate $5,000,000 by age 50 under these assumptions. Now this is a very basic scenario and calculation. However, this is more analysis than most individuals undertake when planning for retirement.

Many individuals feel that if they visit a web site or meet with their financial advisor and run a simple calculation their planning is complete. Regardless of what you may have done, it is important to run sophisticated "what if" scenarios. Most financial calculators assume you will earn your average return of, say 8%, year in and year out. However, many people ignore the fact that the average does not occur each year. What happens when the "averages" are off repeatedly? It is imperative to run different scenarios, such as what happens if you earn one percent less on average.

Additionally, you should run a statistical program sometimes referred to as a Monte Carlo program to examine your results under many different possible annual returns. Monte Carlo software will randomly choose various possible annual returns. Sometimes, the software will run thousands of different return possibilities. You may find under the fixed annual return used by your basic financial calculator, that you will be over funded. However, the Monte Carlo exercise may demonstrate that you have less than a 60% probability of having enough money to fund retirement. The results of this analysis will certainly help determine your final course of action.

Another common mistake is ignoring the burden of taxes. In Fred's case, we failed to evaluate if the $500,000 saved and what portion of the $25,000 annual contribution is tax-deferred. We will take a look at a very simple example of how taxes can erode what you think you can acquire through investment:

Initial Investment	$100,000
Interest rate for 1 year (7%)	$ 7,000
Less Federal Taxes (28%)	$ (1,960)
Net after-tax Investment	$105,040

Another important consideration is inflation. If we factor in a 3% annual inflation rate, the actual total return after taxes and inflation for Fred would be $101,888. ($105,040 x 97%). It is imperative to estimate future income and investment needs in future dollars. A good example of future dollars is to compare what a $35,000 car will cost in 10 years and in 20 years assuming a 4% inflation rate. In 10 years a $35,000 vehicle will cost $51,800 and in 20 years cost $76,700. The effects of inflation must be considered during your planning.

What if you are starting late in the game, and feel you are behind or have made major mistakes?

CLEAR THOUGHT #5

I tell my clients who feel this way to think of the theory of holes:
If you want to get out of a hole, stop digging.

What's important is to take the steps necessary to get yourself on the *right path* to success.

2. Strategy (Everyone Wants to Win on Friday Night)

Some high school football coaches cajole their players into working harder by saying that *everyone wants to win on Friday night.*

The point is that preparation and strategy are key. In reality, most games are won from the hard work put in on the practice field and film room during the week.

There are seven elements to successful strategy formulation and implementation:

1. Situation analysis – Realistically evaluate your current situation as well as your objectives. What stage are you in life? Have you saved something each year since you started working? Are you just now understanding the mistakes you've made and attempting to get yourself on the right path? The situation analysis is like the drawing board for your strategy formulation. This is where the blueprint is conceived and where you look at where you are today and where you want, or need to be in the future.

2. Vision statement or investment policy statement – Use the insights and perspectives generated by your situation analysis as the basis for defining your vision or policy statement. The vision or policy statement defines your goal. The aim is to provide a clear sense of direction that both you and your advisors can understand.

Dennis P. Barba Jr.

3. Issues and alternatives – Now you're ready to make lists of alternatives. All of your alternatives are reviewed and evaluated based on how they will help you achieve your goals.

4. Strategic priorities – You can't always do everything at once. What has the most immediate impact? What is critical in achieving your goals? What will become critical two years from now? You must prioritize the important elements of your plan and set timelines for their completion or implementation.

5. Key changes – What key elements must you change immediately to get on the right path? You may have to make significant alterations in your lifestyle to accomplish your plan. You will probably have to become focused and more disciplined with your finances. Concurrently, the amount of time you commit to your financial future will increase.

6. Alignment or convergence – Your family and all of your key advisors need to be in agreement about your plan.

7. Implementation – Put your plan into action.

Every time you need to assess your progress, NALP will remind you to make sure you are on course toward your ultimate goal.

Dennis P. Barba Jr.

CHAPTER TWO:
Selecting Your Team

Dennis P. Barba Jr.

Selecting Your Team (Reagan vs. Carter)

To effectively put together a financial plan, it's important that you educate yourself as much as possible. Reading books like this one is a good start.

On the other hand, you can't be expected to know everything. To close the gap, remember this Management 101-ism: *Hire quality people, then hold them accountable.*

Consider the track records of Presidents Jimmy Carter and Ronald Reagan. Carter had a reputation for wanting to micro-manage everything. This control-freak management style – perhaps a product of his technical and military training at Annapolis – belied his affable public persona and frustrated cabinet members and staffers.

Reagan, on the other hand, made no apologies for his willingness to delegate. He believed in and trusted his people, and let them do most of the "heavy lifting." (A story goes that Chief of Staff Donald Regan once berated the Gipper prior to a Monday morning staff meeting for not reading a particularly important briefing over the weekend. "Well, Don," Reagan reportedly explained, "The Sound of Music was on last night.")

Two very different management styles, but who was more effective in office? Whatever your political persuasion, you would do better to emulate Reagan when it comes to financial planning. To do this, build a team of key advisors. I recommend having the following advisors as team members:

   – Accountant

   – Financial Advisor

   – Insurance Advisor

   – Estate Planning Attorney

In some cases it may be possible for the same person to advise you in more than one area. For example, some Certified Public Accountants also have law degrees and specialize in tax preparation and estate planning. Many financial advisors are also licensed insurance agents. However, when you have one person perform two functions, be sure that he or she is qualified and experienced in both areas. If an accountant has a law degree but has little experience in complex estate planning, start looking for an estate planning attorney. Many stockbrokers are licensed to sell insurance but have never written a policy.

CLEAR THOUGHT # 6

When selecting your team of advisors, there is no substitute for experience.

The Accountant

Choosing an accountant is one of the most important financial decisions you will make. The right person can add to your sense of security regarding the accuracy of your records. The wrong person can lead you into unnecessarily paying too much in taxes, or, at the other extreme into disputes with the IRS.

Your accountant is the watchdog of your financial planning efforts. Most good accountants have some degree of understanding in estate planning and insurance. Additionally, a good accountant can tell by your year-end statements if your financial advisor knows what he or she is doing. The accountant is a good point person for your financial affairs.

Choosing an accountant is like choosing a roommate. In this case, you are choosing a financial mate. Your accountant will know everything about you, your family, your business, and personal finances. Be sure to choose someone who has your best interests at heart.

Selecting an Accountant:

1. Hire a Certified Public Accountant (CPA), who should be better trained and more experienced than most accountants. To be a CPA, most states require accountants to complete an accounting program at an accredited university and pass a national exam covering a variety of subjects including income tax law, business law, and tax theory.

2. Find an accountant with a solid background and extensive experience in the particular area or areas you need. Make sure he or she has experience in estate planning, retirement planning, and a working knowledge of investments and insurance. A good accountant or tax advisor will help keep you organized, support your financial plan, and assist in your efforts to accumulate and preserve wealth.

3. Make an appointment to meet with the candidates you are considering. Be prepared to explain your needs and what you expect the accountant to do for you and your family. To assess the individual's capability, be sure to ask:

– How long have you been in business?

– What services do you offer?

– What is the composition of your current clientele? Do I fit your profile?

– What are your rates? Will you bill one fee for the year or by the hour? Do you bill for telephone calls?

– Do you have experience representing taxpayers in audits with the IRS?

– What kind of errors and omissions insurance do you carry? What is your policy if you make a mistake in my tax preparation that causes an audit and penalty?

– What information do you expect me to provide and what times during the year do you need this information?

4. Ask for references. However, be careful. Most people obviously will not provide references from unhappy customers. I have found the best references to be from friends. If you don't have a trusted friend for a reference, ask the candidate to provide five to ten references on the spot. If the reply is that they will send a list to you later, be careful. If they truly have a successful practice and an outstanding reputation, they will be able to provide you with references from numerous satisfied customers immediately.

Ultimately, the choice comes down to finding someone who makes you feel comfortable. An accountant can have all the credentials in the world, but if you are not comfortable with the person, then the relationship will never work.

The Financial Advisor

When building a house, the first thing you do, before the chain saw hits the first tree on the lot, is hire an architect.

If a patient is diagnosed with a particular illness, he or she immediately maps out a plan of attack with a physician *before* deciding which treatment options to pursue. If the problem looks serious and the patient is smart, several physicians will be interviewed and a team will be assembled to help fight the disease.

Businesses do not make acquisitions without completing a thorough evaluation of possible candidates and how the potential acquisition fits with the vision and long-term strategy of the company.

In the same way, choosing a financial advisor is a strategic decision, because this person could become one of the key people in your life.

The two most important qualities in a financial advisor are honesty and experience. Most people recognize the importance of honesty, but experience is often overlooked.

You can read every fact about how markets move over time. But when it comes to investing, there is no substitute for experience.

The rookie advisor, with only an academic understanding of the markets, may not know how to react in potentially difficult situations. How would this person handle a customer who is in a panic because the market dropped 15 percent over the last sixty days and a $10 million portfolio is at risk?

Will he panic along with the customer and sell in a bear market in order to avoid uncomfortable confrontations or to generate sales commissions, or will reason prevail?

Can the advisor refer to similar unsettling situations in the past? Will he remind the investor of the importance of staying with the long-term plan?

It amazes me how many people will give large sums of money to stockbrokers, insurance agents, and financial advisors who are new in the business. What do these people *really* know about managing money and risk in volatile markets? Have they actually seen periods of rising interest rates, a weakening dollar, war, falling commodity prices, or high inflation?

Newcomers to this business are really no more than sales executives during the first few years. They are under pressure to produce. They believe what they are told by their sales managers. Under these circumstances, it is extremely difficult for them to concentrate on managing assets for clients. They must bring in new clients and produce revenue to keep their jobs. Given this scenario, it's not surprising that an estimated 60% to 90% of all new financial advisors and stockbrokers leave the business within their first three years.

One of the best ways you learn the financial services business is through your mistakes. Unfortunately, these mistakes that are helpful in the long run are often made at the expense of a client. My advice to any investor is to deal with someone who has been around for a while and seen several market cycles.

CLEAR THOUGHT #7

"There is no substitute for experience"

When the Feeling is Mutual

Experience is particularly important when selecting a mutual fund. If you are purchasing a mutual fund because it has a ten-year track record of a 16% annual return, but the current manager has been running the fund for only eighteen months, you ought to ask yourself if you are doing the right thing. A large part of a fund's management fee presumably buys the experience of the manager. You pay for the privilege of participating in the success of the fund, which is attributable to the fund manager.

The same principles that hold true for your financial advisor apply to mutual fund managers. Buy experience. When markets decline you will be rewarded for the wise choices you made.

Taking this into consideration, how does one go about selecting a stockbroker or financial advisor? The following will help provide you with some guidelines for your selection criteria:

Certified Financial Planner? Insurance professional? Stock broker?

Choose a professional who can offer a broad range of services like those listed below:

– Stock execution and research

– Option execution and strategy, especially for hedging or writing calls

– Corporate, government, and municipal bond execution and strategy

– Mutual fund execution and research (make sure diverse fund families are represented)

– Life insurance, disability insurance, long-term care insurance, and annuity products. (Be sure that a broad range of insurance products are being offered. It is important to deal with someone who can offer several competitive quotes rather than someone tied to one limited product line)

If you are interviewing a stockbroker and he is unable to offer insurance products or financial planning advice, wrap up the interview quickly and move on. Conversely, if you are considering a financial planner or insurance agent and he or she is unable to provide securities execution, equity and economic research, asset allocation expertise, and offer a large selection of mutual fund families, keep looking.

Questions for your Financial Professional

1. What types of services do you provide? Of course, this will depend on what you are looking for. If you want to work with just

one financial professional, find out if the individual can handle all of your needs right away.

2. How many years have you been in the business? What was your previous background, including education? This goes back to the discussion on experience. Beware of inexperienced financial professionals.

3. What registrations or licenses do you have?

4. How do you charge for your services? Do you charge one fee based on the amount of assets under management? Do you have an hourly rate? Do you earn commissions from the products recommended? Discuss all available fee arrangements and negotiate the method that is most comfortable for you.

5. Will you review my portfolio on a regular basis? How often will we meet to discuss my financial situation? Is there a charge for these meetings?

6. Do you provide a newsletter or conduct client seminars?

7. What research facilities does your firm make available to customers? How do you receive information on equities and investment strategies? How does the information you receive set you apart from everyone else?

8. Do you work with people who have profiles similar to mine? Do I fit the profile of your typical client? How would I stand relative to your top-tier clients? Would I receive the same attention as your top 20%? (This is very important. In the financial services industry, 80% of a firm's revenue is generated from 20% of their clients. It is important to deal with someone who believes you will be, or have the potential to be, one of his or her top 20%. You stand a much greater chance of receiving top-tier attention if you are valuable to your advisor).

The Estate-Planning Attorney

The third member of your team is your estate-planning attorney. Without considerable planning and attention, taxes can significantly reduce the value of the proceeds passed on to your heirs.

Proper planning and coordination with an estate planning professional can help ensure that your heirs receive the estate you intended them to have. Improper or misguided planning may be little better than no action at all, allowing unnecessary probate expenses and taxes to erode the value of your estate.

CLEAR THOUGHT #8

If you are married and have a net worth in excess of $1,000,000 or are single with a net worth in excess of $650,000, start proper estate planning *now*.

Lawyers intimidate most people. They make the mistake of thinking that all attorneys are aggressive, that they overcharge, and ultimately will take control of their assets. This is simply not the case.

The most important qualities to look for in your estate-planning attorney are experience and specialization. You should hire an attorney who has been practicing for at least five years, and more importantly, one who specializes in estate planning. If you are worried about an attorney's past, you can check on his disciplinary history by contacting the Bar Association in your area.

Your Insurance Professional

No one likes writing checks to an insurance company. Unfortunately, it is a necessity. Your insurance professional should specialize not only in property and casualty insurance, but also life, disability, long-term care, and have a basic knowledge of estate planning. Additionally, deal with an insurance professional that represents multiple carriers. Many times, Independent agents representing many different insurance companies can provide more competitive quotes than an agent representing a single carrier. Additionally, one carrier may offer a more competitive rate on life insurance, while another carrier is more competitive in property and casualty insurance. An agent representing multiple carries can shop for the best price in each insurance category and handle the administration and customer service from their agency office. However, make certain your agent is properly equipped to handle customer service. Pay a visit to the office and meet the staff. Review their agency customer service policy to determine if it matches your needs.

Using one advisor for multiple functions

In some instances, you may want to consider using one key advisor for more than one aspect of your plan. My experience has demonstrated that the following relationships can work:

Accounting and estate planning

If an individual is an accountant and also an attorney specializing in estate planning, it makes sense to use one person for both functions. However, I do not recommend letting an accountant or estate-planning lawyer handle your investments. Some accountants have become registered as financial planners. It is simply too time-consuming and difficult to keep abreast of all the tax law changes and at the same time be able to follow the financial markets. In many cases, an accountant will not have access to all the products and services available to a full-service brokerage firm, bank, or large-scale financial planner.

Insurance planning and investment planning

If your financial advisor wants to handle your insurance planning or vice versa, be sure he or she has the proper experience and specialization in both areas. Additionally, be sure you will receive quotes from several top-rated insurance companies and also have access to all products and services available in the financial markets. Many insurance professionals have access to mutual funds and annuities, but not to individual stock, bond, and option research and execution.

After you have chosen your team and are ready to begin the planning process, the next concern is how much? What are the fees you will incur to put your plan in place?

CLEAR THOUGHT #9

Regarding fees:

First, Everything is negotiable.

Second, You get what you pay for.

It is certainly acceptable to negotiate a fee for accounting, legal, or financial services to a level that is acceptable to both yourself and the professional planner. In fact, far too many people are probably paying more than they should for their professional advice. They are simply too intimidated to ask for a better rate.

On the other hand, if the professional believes the most important thing on your mind is the fee, he may not want to do business with you. If you are determined to retain one of the top professionals in your area, expect to pay for his or her expertise and enhanced service. You want to ensure that your newly hired professional will give you the quality service you desire and the same service consistently provided to all other clients.

CHAPTER THREE:
The Planning Process

Dennis P. Barba Jr.

Financial Planning

What is financial planning? What does it encompass? Today, retirement is on many people's minds – whether young or old.

With continuing advances in science and medicine, lifespans are becoming longer. Someone who is now sixty-five can expect to live to the age of eighty-two. Additionally, the elderly of today are enjoying a better quality of life. This enhanced lifestyle comes with additional costs. It takes money to remain active, hence the importance of good financial planning.

Financial planning combines the following areas:

– Retirement planning

– Investment planning

– Asset Allocation

– College funding

– Major purchase savings

– Risk management (life, health, disability insurance)

– Income tax strategies

– Estate planning

If your planning is thorough and well implemented, it will provide you with peace of mind, and with answers to the following questions:

– Do I have enough money to retire when I want and to live the lifestyle I desire?

– Will my assets sustain me?

– Will I have money left over to leave my heirs?

– What effects will taxes have upon my plans?

– Have I invested properly?

– Have I done everything I can to plan for my future?

There are many reasons for planning:

– To achieve a comfortable retirement.

– To meet future college expenses.

– To protect your family and assets in the event that you lose your job, become disabled, or die.

– To ensure that your estate is managed appropriately and is not subject to unnecessary settlement expenses and taxation.

– To use insurance to mitigate risk when possible.

CLEAR THOUGHT #10

If you have a financial plan, you are far more likely to achieve your goals.

"Can you please tell me, Cheshire Cat," asked Alice, "which direction I ought to go?"

"That depends," said the Cat, "on where it is you want to be."

– Lewis Carroll

CLEAR THOUGHT #11

"If you don't know where you are going, you are already lost"

This is where NALP returns to the picture. Ironically the place to start planning is at the end: what is your final, ultimate goal?

To do this, we have to determine how much money and income you will need when you retire. However, it is difficult to ascertain what your end need is without examining your current situation. This is where you take inventory of your current income and expenses and your current assets and liabilities. The situation analysis begins with these questions:

- What is your current income?
- What are your current expenses?
- What discretionary income do you have available to invest for retirement?
- How much have you saved so far?
- How much money do you owe to others?

Review your current income and expenses. You need to be aware of all the details so I recommend the following:

1. Write down your current income

Analyze your cash flow for the last twelve months and project what it will be for the next year. Be sure to include the following when estimating your monthly income:

- Wages, salary, tips
- Alimony, child support
- Dividends from stocks and mutual funds
- Interest from savings accounts, checking accounts, money market accounts, bonds, CDs, etc.
- Social security benefits
- Pension checks
- Royalties

- Rental income
- Any other income

2. List your annual expenses in detail.

Be sure to arrive at a true figure, not just what you think your monthly budget might be. The following is a guideline for calculating your true expense, which most people tend to *underestimate*:

- Mortgage payment and property taxes
- Insurance premiums for all categories
- Educational expenses
- Auto payments, insurance, and repairs
- Landscaping for your home
- Home upkeep. How much do you actually spend each year on repairs or updating your home?
- Club dues, association dues, professional dues
- Hobbies
- Subscriptions
- Gifts to church or charities
- Gifts to relatives and friends for birthdays, holidays, and special occasions
- Assistance with children or parents
- Taxes
- Accountants and lawyers fees
- Clothing expenses
- Food
- Dining out
- Cleaning supplies
- Taking care of your pets
- Vacations
- Gas

– Utilities including cell phones, electric, water, gas, etc.

– "Walking around" money

– Debt service

– Student loans

– Alimony and child support

Look at your bank and credit card statements and calculate what you really spent for the past year. Can you accurately determine where your money went? Most of us have absolutely no idea!

When you go to a financial professional for advice, one of the first things he will need to know is how much money you actually spend and actually earn.

After you calculate your monthly income and expenses, you can determine how much discretionary income you have available after your monthly obligations are met. Keep this information handy because you will need to refer to it later when you attempt to figure out exactly what you will need on a monthly basis for retirement.

3. Net Worth

The second part of the situation analysis is to determine your net worth.

Just as corporations must prepare a balance sheet and report to their bankers and shareholders their current net worth, individuals should also have a personal balance sheet. The following will provide a good working outline:

Assets

Tangible Assets:

- Residence

- Second residence

- Rental properties

- Home furnishings

- Automobiles

- Art, jewelry or collectibles

- Other personal property

Equity Assets:

- Stocks

- Mutual funds

- Variable annuities

- Limited Partnerships

Business Ownership:

- Ownership in a personal business

- Equity in business real estate

- Equity in business insurance policies

Dennis P. Barba Jr.

Debt Assets:

- Bonds including government, foreign, corporate, and municipal
- Closed-end and open-end bond funds
- Personal loans made to friends and family
- Loans made to your business

Cash and Liquid Assets:

- Checking accounts
- Savings Accounts
- Money Market Accounts
- CDs
- Other Cash Reserves
- Cash Value in insurance policies

Debt

Liabilities:

- Home mortgage
- Vacation home mortgage
- Rental or investment properties mortgages
- Auto loans
- Student loans
- Bank loans
- Credit card loans
- Business loans
- Secured loans
- Other debts

Total Net Worth

Total Assets: $_____

Minus Total Liabilities: $_____

= Net Worth: $_____

4. Vision Statement (I Can See Clearly Now)

The first part of our strategic financial formula was the situation analysis. Having completed that, we now know how much you make, how much you have, and how much you owe. Now create a vision of where you want and need to be in the future. The vision statement is your view of the future.

But remember what your parents told you: There is a difference between your needs and your wants.

You will *need* to be able to afford to pay your utility bills, provide for adequate health insurance, have your home paid off or have enough money to pay rent. Conversely, you may *want* to travel the world, own a second home, and send your grandchildren to college.

I have found it most productive to plan for the lifestyle you want and determine if these goals are financially obtainable. If your ideal retirement desires are out of line with your income you should re-evaluate your strategy. This method will allow you to paint an accurate picture of your future needs.

During this part of the planning process you will estimate what your monthly expenses will be when you retire and the source of your income.

When determining this figure you should refer back to the worksheet used to calculate your current monthly expenses.

Examine each category and decide what you would expect to spend in **today's dollars** when you retire. For example, you may substitute house payment and education expenses with travel and medical expenses. It can be difficult to predict how you will want to live ten or twenty years from now. However, it is necessary to begin thinking about this subject realistically when you start planning.

Your Retirement Tools

After the stock market crash of 1929 and the Great Depression, the public turned to the government to ensure that no one would have to live their "golden" years in poverty. The United States government's solution was the Social Security Act of 1935.

However, now that the baby boomers are approaching retirement age, Social Security is showing signs of strain. By approximately 2012, Social Security will be paying out more in retirement benefits than it takes in from payroll taxes. Additionally, only 23% of an average person's retirement income comes from Social Security.

A number of "tools" can help with your retirement planning. Many have tax advantages. Check with your tax or financial advisor to investigate your eligibility for each program. Be sure to ask your employer about the plans the company offers. When you invest in an individual retirement account or employer-sponsored plan, all dividends, interest, and capital gains accumulate in your account on a tax-deferred basis until you withdraw the money—usually during retirement, when your income may be subject to a lower tax rate. Meanwhile, your reinvested earnings generate more earnings, and so on.

Individual Tools

Traditional Individual Retirement Account (IRA)

An IRA offers the ability to contribute up to $2,000 annually into a retirement account. With a traditional IRA, your contributions grow tax-deferred. Depending on whether you are an active participant in an employer-sponsored retirement plan and also on your adjusted gross income, the deduction may be full or partially deductible from your taxable income.

However, if you withdraw funds before age 59-1/2, the money is subject to regular taxation as well as a 10% penalty. If you continue to work well into your sixties or need only a portion of your IRA balance to supplement your income, you must consider the impact of minimum distribution requirements enforced by the IRS. You must take minimum distributions by April 1st of the year after you reach 70-1/2. If the IRS schedule is not followed, there can be a 50% penalty on the minimum amount you should have withdrawn.

Although the benefits of tax deferral are significant, traditional IRA's have drawbacks. The following highlight some benefits and drawbacks of traditional IRA's:

Benefits of Traditional IRA's

– **Tax Deferral.** Investment earnings compound tax-free. This allows your IRA to grow faster than it would if it were subject to annual taxes on income and capital gains.

– **Flexibility.** You may invest your traditional IRA assets in virtually any type of mutual fund, or in other securities offered through banks or brokerage firms.

– **Tax Deduction.** Your contributions may be tax-deductible if you are not an active participant in an employer-sponsored plan (such as a 401(k) plan) or if your adjusted gross income is below a certain level. For 2001, the threshold is $33,000 for single filers and $53,000 for joint filers. For 2001, partial deductions are allowed on incomes up to $43,000 for single filers and $63,000 for joint filers.

Drawbacks of Traditional IRAs

– Various Penalties. You could be penalized if you withdraw your money before age 59-1/2, depending on the circumstances of your withdrawal. You'll also pay a penalty if you contribute more than $2,000 a year (or 100% of your earned income, whichever is less) or don't withdraw enough after age 70-1/2.

– Ultimate Tax Consequences. Your IRA's aren't entirely insulated from taxes. When you ultimately withdraw funds, you'll pay ordinary income tax on your investment earnings (and on any deductible contribution amounts). Remember that tax deferral can offset much of the taxes paid at withdrawal.

It is imperative to consult with a professional to determine your projected minimum distributions and how they will affect your tax situation. Additionally, upon the death of the recipient and beneficiary, the balance in an IRA can be subject to both income tax and estate taxes. It is also crucial to consult with an expert when designating a beneficiary when rolling your retirement plan into an IRA. In January of 2001, the IRS issued new proposed regulations that may simplify the minimum distribution calculation, starting with the 2001 distributions. You should check with a professional to determine how these proposed changes may relate to your situation.

Roth IRA

In 1998, Congress elected to establish a tax-advantaged investment alternative called the Roth IRA.

A Roth IRA is funded with after-tax dollars. As with the traditional IRA, you may still contribute up to $2,000 each year. To be eligible to contribute the full $2,000, you must be a single tax filer with an adjusted gross income below $95,000 or a married couple with an adjusted income below $150,000. Partial contributions are permitted for individuals with adjusted gross incomes between $95,000 and $110,000, and for AGI between $150,000 and $160,000 for married couples. The earnings in a Roth IRA are not taxed as they grow and distributions are tax-free, as long as you have had the account for five years and meet restrictions governing withdrawal.

To qualify for a tax-free withdrawal from your Roth IRA at age 59-1/2 a distribution has to be made after a five-year holding period. Additionally, tax-free withdrawals can be made after the five-year holding period due to death or disability or for the purchase of your first home subject to certain limitations.

Finally, you are eligible to roll your traditional IRA into a Roth IRA to avoid taxes on further growth. It is wise to consult with a professional to determine if this strategy is appropriate for your situation. Generally, you can convert your traditional IRA to a Roth IRA if you file a single or joint tax return reporting an AGI of $100,000 or less for the tax year of the conversion. Keep in mind, however, that you'll owe taxes (but no penalty) on the conversion. If you withdraw money from a converted Roth IRA within the first five years of the conversion, you will generally owe a 10% penalty tax on the taxable amount of your withdrawal. Under certain circumstances, you could also face an accelerated income tax bill. It is critical to seek professional advice prior to converting an Individual Retirement Account into a Roth IRA.

The following outline some benefits and drawbacks to Roth IRA's:

– **Tax Deferral.** As with a traditional IRA, your investment earnings compound tax-free.

– **Tax-Free Withdrawal.** Unlike a traditional IRA, the Roth IRA lets you withdraw your earnings tax-free if you are at least 59-

1/2 years old and your account has been established for at least five years.

– **Flexibility.** Like a traditional IRA, you may invest your Roth IRA assets in virtually any type of mutual fund or securities offered by banks and brokerage firms.

Drawbacks of Roth IRAs

– **Various Penalties.** As with a traditional IRA, you'll pay a penalty with a Roth IRA in certain cases. For example, you may be penalized if you withdraw your earnings before age 59-1/2 or contribute more than $2,000 a year (or 100% of your earned income, whichever is less). Unlike a traditional IRA, however, a Roth IRA does not require you to take minimum distributions after age 70-1/2.

– **Tax Issues.** Contributions to a Roth IRA do not qualify for an up-front tax deduction. When you convert a traditional IRA to a Roth IRA, you must pay ordinary income tax on the converted amount that represents deductible contributions and earnings. As a result, IRA conversions are attractive to investors who expect their tax rate to be higher in retirement than it is today.

Annuities

An annuity is another type of tax-deferred investment vehicle. It is not technically a retirement plan. An annuity is a contract between an investor and an insurance company. Unlike the $2,000 annual contribution limit to an IRA, an annuity allows you to make unlimited contributions, subject to the provisions of the insurance contract. The investor makes a deposit of funds and earnings have the potential to grow within the contract on a tax-deferred basis. Earnings on the premium are not taxed until they are withdrawn.

Unlike the traditional IRA, the original contribution is not subject to income tax at death since the contributions generally come from after-tax dollars. However, annuities can be subject to the same 10% penalty if funds are removed prior to age 59-1/2.

Types of Annuities

There are two very common types of annuities: fixed and variable. The primary difference is how the potential increase in value of the annuity contract occurs. The increase can be a fixed return or a variable rate of return.

A fixed annuity is issued a fixed interest rate for a specific time period. The rate can stay fixed for the length of the contract or can be adjusted periodically. With a fixed annuity, the insurance company guarantees a minimum rate specified in the annuity contract and the rate and principal are guaranteed. However, this guarantee is only as strong as the underlying insurance company. Beware of fixed annuity offers that sound too good to be true. It is important to know the financial stability of the issuing company.

During the past decade, variable annuities have become increasing popular. According to the National Association for Variable Annuities, the number of sub accounts increased from 175 in 1987 to over 3,000 in 1997. Unlike fixed annuities, the insurance company does not guarantee variable contracts. They are in many ways similar to mutual funds in that the performance of the contract is dependent upon the underlying securities chosen for investment. In fact, in many contracts the investor has the option of choosing well-known mutual funds for the sub-accounts. The performance of a variable annuity will fluctuate according to how you allocate your premiums. Investors can usually choose from a variety of investment options according to the individual risk profile and objectives of the investor. The investor has control of how the premiums are allocated.

Choosing a fixed or variable annuity will depend on many factors including your:

- Age
- Tolerance for volatility
- Allocation preferences
- Investment objectives
- Investment horizon
- Targeted return objective

Annuity distributions

There are options to consider when deciding to take distributions from an annuity. Distributions can be taken as a lump sum or over a series of payments. Often, investors choose to take their distribution in payments over a period of time. If you exercise this· option you may be able to choose between three different options:

- Single life
- Specified period or period certain
- Joint and survivor

Once again, it is crucial to consult with a qualified professional when making a choice between fixed and variable annuities and deciding how to take distributions.

Corporate Tools

There are two broad categories of employer-sponsored retirement plans: Defined benefit plans, and defined contribution plans. About one-half of U.S. workers are covered by an employer-sponsored plan. If you work for a large or midsize company, you are probably eligible to participate in such a plan. Even if you work for a smaller organization, there are options available to employers to offer a retirement savings vehicle. It is surpassing how many people who are eligible for an employer-sponsored retirement actually participate:

> *– 57% of eligible employees actually participate*
>
> *– 24% make some contributions*
>
> *– 15% make the maximum contribution*
>
> **Source: USA Today snapshots, USA Today, March 12, 1996*

Defined Benefit Plans

Defined benefit plans are the traditional company-sponsored retirement plans. Typically, they pay a defined pension or retirement benefit. This benefit is typically based on your salary before retirement, as well as your total years of service. Under Defined Benefit Plans:

- Your employer makes the contributions.
- The Internal Revenue Service limits the amount of annual pension benefits you can receive. For 2001, the limit is the lesser of $140,000 or 100% of your average annual pay during your 3 highest consecutive salary years.
- In most cases, pension benefits are guaranteed up to a certain monthly limit by a government agency known as the Pension Benefit Guaranty Corporation.

Defined Contribution Plans

Defined contribution plans have become increasingly popular as companies have migrated from the traditional defined benefit plans.

Under Defined Contribution Plans:

– You are not promised a set benefit or pension at retirement. Alternatively, an individual account is established in your name, and your retirement benefits depend on how much is contributed and the rate of return earned by the account's investments.

– The IRS limits the annual contributions that can be made on your behalf. For 2001, the limit is the lesser of $35,000 or 25% of your total compensation.

– The federal government does not guarantee these benefits. Conversely, these plans allow you choose from among several investment options. You, then, are responsible for ensuring that your investments provide adequate returns to meet your retirement needs.

Many large companies offering a defined benefit plan also offer a defined contribution plan as a supplement to their employees' retirement savings.

What if you are a small business owner or work for a smaller company? Many smaller companies sponsor one or more defined contribution plans. These plans are far more cost effective for the company than the traditional defined benefit plan. The following outlines some common types of defined contribution plans:

Profit-sharing plan: Employer contributes and can determine how much, if any, to contribute each year. Contributions typically are based on each employee's current-year compensation.

Money purchase plan: Employer contributes and must provide a fixed amount (or percentage of compensation) each year for each participating employee. Contributions may exceed those allowed with profit-sharing plans.

Thrift (or savings) plan: Both employer and employees contribute, and employer matches all or a fraction of employees' contributions. (For example, an employer may contribute 25 percent of the contributions an employee makes into the plan).

Employee stock ownership plan (ESOP): Employer contributes shares of the company's stock to employees.

401(k) plan: The most popular variation of profit-sharing/thrift plan. Employees make regular, pretax contributions through payroll deductions, and employers may match some portion of employees' contributions.

403(b) plan: Variation of profit-sharing/thrift plan for employees of public schools and tax-exempt organizations. Work similar to a 401(k) plan, but by law offers only two funding arrangements: an annuity contract with an insurance company, and a custodial account in mutual funds (403[b][7] account).

Keogh plan: Self-employed individuals contribute, according to rules much like those for a qualified large-company plan.

Nonqualified deferred compensation plan: Employers contribute, generally on behalf of highly paid employees to supplement qualified plans. Does not meet IRS rules for qualified plans (e.g., may not be funded to ensure future benefits, and funds may not be shielded from creditors).

Understanding your employer-sponsored plan will help you make the most of your benefits. You should consult with your financial advisor to review your employer-sponsored retirement plans and to be certain you are making the maximum contributions affordable, and that your contributions are properly allocated.

CLEAR THOUGHT #12

Be sure to take maximum advantage of employer-sponsored retirement plans and make the maximum contribution you can afford.

Dennis P. Barba Jr.

I have run into instances where a client works for a company that matches dollar for dollar on the first 3% of what employees contribute to their 401K plan, yet the employee does not participate. When asked why they respond, "I haven't got around to it yet." How much would this cost this individual say, over three years of missed contributions and company matching?

Salary	$75,000
3% of salary	$ 2,250
100% company match	$ 2,250

If a 35 year-old waits just three years to participate in this employer-sponsored plan, he will forgo in excess of $120,000 at retirement assuming an 8% annualized rate of return.

Insurance Tools

– Insurance, or risk management, is an important component of any financial plan. Again, when selecting an insurance professional, seek someone with ample experience and who specializes in estate-planning insurance. We will talk about five basic types of insurance:

- **Property and Casualty insurance**
- **Life insurance**
- **Disability insurance**
- **Long-term care insurance**
- **The umbrella policy**

You will need an agent who is familiar with the above-mentioned areas of insurance coverage.

It's wise to shop around for your property and casualty insurance, and to use an agent for your life, disability, and long-term care needs. Find an agent who can provide quotes from several different insurance underwriters or carriers. You are more likely to receive the best price if you can choose from several different companies, rather than being locked into one carrier.

What to consider in insurance planning

Be sure to consider the following areas when planning your insurance coverage:

1. Property and casualty: Are you adequately insured for your residence and automobiles? Are you protected in the event of an injury at your home or in a devastating auto accident? Do you have an umbrella policy to protect yourself from sizeable lawsuits that may occur? Do you have riders to cover any jewelry, collectibles, or other valuable items, which may not be covered under your homeowner's policy? Do you have replacement value insurance for your home and its contents?

2. Umbrella Policies: Basically, umbrella policies sit on top of other insurance that includes liability protection, such as homeowners, auto and boat policies. When your primary insurance is not enough, the umbrella policy is triggered, spreading its protection (hence the term "umbrella"). Umbrella policies typically cover you and family members who live with you for accidental injuries to another person or another person's property. The smallest policies (and the most common) pay up to $1 million per incident beyond what's covered by the underlying policy. If you have $300,000 of personal liability protection on your auto policy and a $1 million umbrella policy, under most policies you would have a total of $1.3 million worth of insurance standing between an injured party and your assets. The easiest way to buy an umbrella policy is through the same company that handles your homeowners or auto insurance. Insurance companies also require that you maintain certain minimum levels of liability coverage on the underlying policies. You will have to check with your agent. Umbrella polices begin to protect you after your basic liability levels are exceeded.

Let's take a moment to address some confusion regarding umbrella policies.

– It's just for the rich.
– It's too complicated to coordinate with your existing insurance like your homeowner's policy.
– The premiums are too expensive.

Not true. Umbrella coverage is very affordable, can be easily coordinated with your existing insurance policies and is in no way designed for the rich. In fact, any good insurance agent should present this option.

Some examples of where umbrella coverage often comes into play:

– An auto accident in which you're sued under your auto insurance policy.
– Your neighbor falls on your property, and you're sued under your homeowner's insurance.
– A natural disaster in which another person's property is damaged by a tree on your property crashing down on their vehicle or home. This usually falls into the, "I thought that was covered by my homeowner's policy" category.

Your auto and homeowner's policies have at least some liability insurance that would be used to settle legal claims. But what if a settlement (or judgment, if it goes to court) is $800,000 and you only have $300,000 of liability insurance? The insurer would pay its $300,000, but where are you going to get the other $500,000)? Why risk what you have accumulated?

With the litigious society in which we live, you can't afford not to have umbrella liability insurance.

Umbrella liability insurance pays $1 million, $2 million and sometimes even $5 million or more of a claim, on top of what your basic policies will pay. You're usually able to set the amount. For the protection you get, umbrella liability coverage is not very expensive. Premiums are usually $200 to $300 a year for $1 million worth of coverage. Your premium will depend on such criteria as the amount of coverage, the insurance company issuing the policy and your own "personal risk factors" (such as the number of traffic tickets you've gotten in the past few years).

When people do buy, they often don't buy enough. For example, you may have assets worth $1 million, figure that you need enough coverage to protect your assets, and therefore buy a $1 million policy. But what if a judgment of $2 million is handed down? Not only are your assets at risk. Your future income, if you have to make settlement payments over time, could be jeopardized. Likewise, any inheritance you may receive could possibly be seized for payment.

How much you own is irrelevant when deciding how much to purchase. Do you live in a wealthy town, where you could be an easy target for a big settlement? Do you travel a lot? Do you entertain a lot? Do you operate a home-based business and have employees or clients coming to your home on a regular basis? (Many self-employed people wrongly assume that this is covered in their homeowner's policy). If you answered yes to any of these questions, it is particularly important for you to have umbrella liability insurance.

Umbrella coverage, if nothing else, offers psychological comfort. You'll know that if your neighbor falls on your front steps or you rear-end the car in front of you that you're protected from unexpected litigation.

Dennis P. Barba Jr.

CLEAR THOUGHT #13

Be certain to take advantage of an Umbrella Policy from your property and casualty carrier. This is a premium worth paying.

2. Disability insurance: What happens if you become disabled and are unable to work? Will you be able to meet your monthly living expenses? Many of us have disability policies at work. If you read the fine print, some of these policies are not what they seem to be. Additionally, if you lose your job, you may loose your disability insurance. It makes sense to review your company disability policy with your insurance professional and determine whether it provides you with adequate coverage and if you need an additional policy.

3. Long-term care insurance: Long-term care refers to a wide range of health, social and/or personal care services designed to help individuals who need continued help with activities of daily living due to physical or congenital impairment. The following table will demonstrate some of these needs:

Activities of daily living	Long-term services
Bathing	Nursing home
Dressing	Nursing home
Eating	Nursing home
Toileting	Hospice facility
Transferring	assisted living facility
Continence	Alzheimer's centers

The average person often overlooks long-term care insurance. Let's take a look at how the risk of needing long-term care or the services of a nursing home compares to other common risks.

For every 1,000 people:

– Five will have a house fire with an average loss of $3,428.

– Seventy will have an auto accident with an average loss of $3,000.

– 600 will need long-term care with an average cost of $30,000-$80,000 each year.

According to 1997 market research figures, the average costs for daily nursing home care range from $94.00 to over $200.00 per day, depending on where you live.

You should have long-term care insurance if you:

– Have at least $100,000 in assets.

– Are relatively healthy (anyone with degenerative disorders will not be considered for long-term care).

– Wish to preserve financial independence and avoid having to rely on others.

– Have control in choosing the type of care needed and be able to afford services.

– Need to safeguard retirement savings.

– Want to avoid depending on Medicare.

These are the most common mistakes people make when considering long-term care insurance:

– **Assuming Medicare supplement will pay**: Medicare covers only about 17.8% of the total long-term care costs in the United States.

– **Medicaid will cover me**: With respect to long-term care, Medicaid should only be considered as a last resort. As an important part of the welfare system Medicaid has, from its inception, required that its recipients be impoverished. In other words, you have to plan to go broke by spending down your assets to state and federal Medicaid guidelines. In addition, divesting assets intentionally for this purpose may be illegal in many instances.

– I will never need long-term care: All of us hope we will never need long-term care, but the fact is, nearly half of all people over age sixty-five will need long-term care at some point.

– I will pay the cost of long-term care myself: With annual nursing home costs averaging $40,000–$70,000 every year, how long will you be able to afford this type of care? Half of all married couples have spent most of their assets within a year after one of them enters a nursing home.

– My spouse or children will take care of me: Although your spouse or children may want to take care of you, will they be able to afford it for any length of time?

– I am too young: The best time to buy insurance is when you are young and in good health. If you wait too long, the premiums will be higher and you may loose qualification due to failing health. The longer you wait the more it will cost.

Life insurance coverage

What happens if you die? What happens if you your spouse dies? Will the survivor and family members be able to enjoy the same lifestyle they have now? This is a question too often left unanswered. Most of us delay thinking about death as long as possible. Additionally, I have heard many husbands say they have adequate life insurance coverage through work, or that their wife and children could survive comfortably with his $500,000 in coverage. Is this necessarily correct? Many couples fail to find out until it's too late.

You must do some careful analysis and planning when deciding whether you have enough coverage to protect your family.

First, closely examine your coverage at work. In most cases this coverage is quite affordable. Additionally, in most cases you are covered by a term insurance policy. These policies are usually portable if you leave the company, meaning you can convert your policy to an individual policy from your group plan and pay for it on your own after you have resigned or been let go. However, in many cases the conversion costs for these policies are exorbitant. Often, a terminated employee may not be able to afford the premiums to continue the policy. If this happens, you will have to purchase insurance on your own.

What if you are in bad health and are uninsurable? It is critical to have enough insurance coverage for your family outside of your employer's plan if conversion is expensive.

Think of the following example when deciding what insurance coverage is the right amount for your family. Let's look at another case study.

The John Doe Family

John Doe is a 42-year-old executive at a food service company with an annual salary of $250,000. Family circumstances are outlined as follows:

- Jane Doe is a stay at home mom.
- The Doe's have three children ages three, eight and twelve.
- The two oldest attend private school for a annual combined cost of $12,000.
- They intend on sending the youngest child to private school.
- The Doe's own a home valued at $400,000 with a $275,000 mortgage.

Dennis P. Barba Jr.

- Their monthly mortgage payment is $2,500 per month including insurance and taxes.
- The Does owe $25,000 of credit card debt and $40,000 on Jane's student loans from college.
- The Does have $835 each month in auto lease payments.
- The Does currently spend $2,500 per month on living expenses to maintain their current lifestyle.
- John has a $500,000 insurance policy at work and an additional $100,000 policy he purchased when he got married.

John thinks he has adequate coverage should he die.

Is he correct?

Let's examine the debts of the Doe family:

– Mortgage balances	$275,000
– Credit Card debt	$ 25,000
– Student Loan debt	$ 40,000
Total debt	**$ 340,000**

Now, let's examine the assets available for investment of the Doe family:

– Equities and Mutual Funds	$150,000
– 401K plan at work	$100,000
Total assets	**$250,000**

The Doe family appears to have enough insurance coverage to pay off their house and all debts, should John pass away. However, John states that he wants his family to enjoy the same standard of living should he pass away and would not want his wife to have to sell their house or have to take their children out of private school.

Do the Does have enough coverage to accomplish this goal?

Monthly expenses after John's death (after tax)

House Payment	$ 0.00
House taxes	400.00
Tuition	1,000.00
One car payment	400.00
Utilities	500.00
Insurance premiums	275.00
House repairs	200.00
Clothing/laundry	300.00
Food	850.00
Child Care	100.00
Hobbies	200.00
Medical expenses	100.00
Dining out	400.00
Recreation/travel	200.00
Professional services	50.00
Charitable contributions	50.00
Holiday/birthday gifts	200.00
Other expenses	300.00
Total monthly expenses	**$5,525.00**

When John dies, Jane and the kids will have $410,000 from which to draw an income from.

Insurance Proceeds	$600,000
Less Debt Repayment	–$340,000
Plus Equities & Mutual Funds	$150,000
TOTAL	**$410,000**

– The family will not initially use the $100,000 401(K) plan, as they will not wish to pay the taxes due.

As we can see from the example above, the family will need $5,525 per month after taxes, or approximately $85,000 annually in pre-tax income to maintain their current lifestyle.

We need to keep in mind that Jane will have one more child to send to private school and three kids to put through college. Additionally, Jane has no plans to go back to work.

If Jane thinks she could earn a 7% annualized rate of return on her funds, she would generate approximately $28,700 in pre-tax income. Obviously, this would not be enough to allow her to lead the lifestyle she and her children are currently experiencing. In fact, she would be devastated financially.

Therefore, we can conclude that John Doe is underinsured, but by how much?

Let's look at how Jane's expenses will grow over time with inflation. To repeat, Jane has three children to put through college. She has decided she wants to send the children to a private university, similar to the one she and her husband attended. The average price (in today's dollars) of a private university in her state is $18,000 with room and board. We must also factor in the future cost of the educational expenses.

We will use a 3% inflation rate on expenses and a 3% inflation rate on college expenses for this illustration.

The projected college costs when each child turns eighteen will be as follows:

12 year old	$86,000 for four years
8 year old	$91,000 for four years
3 year old	$112,000 for four years

Total amount needed for college education $289,000

Jane would need approximately $2,000,000 today to live according to the standards discussed above. Therefore, John Doe is underinsured by at least $1,500,000.

CLEAR THOUGHT# 14

Make sure you have adequate insurance coverage to protect your family in the event of your death.

CHAPTER FOUR:
Educational Planning

Educational Planning Tools

Another common mistake is not planning for college expenses. Saving for college has always been a challenge for families. College costs have historically increased at a much greater pace than inflation. Additionally, it is now common for most kids to take five years to graduate from college. This just ads to the financial burden placed on the parents or the child in the form of student loan debt after graduation.

There are 4 basic types of college savings plans available today:

1. Custodial Accounts (UGMA/UTMA)

2. Educational IRA

3. Prepaid Tuition Programs

4. 529 College Savings Plans

Custodial Accounts.

A custodial account is opened in the name of a minor under the Uniform Gifts to Minors Act (UGMA) or the Uniform Transfers to Minors Act (UTMA). The type of account varies by state. In a custodial account, taxes are determined based on the child's earnings and exemptions and all or a portion may be taxed at the child's lower marginal rate, which means college savings have the opportunity to compound at a faster rate.

Custodial accounts are irrevocable gifts to minors and the assets will belong to the child regardless of whether the child actually goes to college. The custodian controls the account for the minor until the age of majority, usually 18. The money in this type of account must be used for the benefit of the minor. Many firms closely monitor withdrawals from UGMA's to be certain the funds are in fact being used for the minor.

There are no annual contribution limits, however a married couple can only contribute $20,000 per year as a couple to a UGTMA account without having to file a gift tax return.

Assuming the child is under age 14, the first $750 in income falls into the child's zero tax bracket. The next $750 of income is taxed at a rate of 15%. The balance of income may be subject to tax at the parent's top bracket. If your child is over the age of 14, all income will be taxed at the child's tax rate.

Educational IRA

The Educational IRA is a non-deductible IRA used for college educational expenses. This type of account is good for parents looking to save a small amount each year for their children and have the earnings grow tax exempt.

The maximum contribution permitted in an Educational IRA is $500 per year per child. There are also income limitations placed on the parents. The Educational IRA is limited to taxpayers with adjusted gross income (AGI) under $110,000 for single taxpayers, and $160,000 for couples filing joint returns.

Earnings in Educational IRA's typically accrue tax exempt. However, should you withdraw funds for a non-qualified expense, a 10% penalty on earnings is assessed..

Section 529 College Savings Plans

The introduction of state-sponsored college savings plans prompted federal tax legislation in 1997 known as Section 529 of the Internal Revenue (IRS) Code. 529 Plans offer advantages to families wishing to save for college.

Dennis P. Barba Jr.

Nearly 40 states now offer 529 Plans. Most state's plans differ, so check with your advisor when investigating 529 plans in your state. There are several features most 529 plans have in common. First, 529 plans provide earnings deferred from taxes from inception until funds are withdrawn to pay for college. When withdrawn, earnings are taxed at the child's rate instead of the parent's rate.

Secondly, if the funds are not used for education expenses, the earnings will be subject to a penalty between 10%-15%, in addition to regular taxation. However, should the child receive a scholarship, the amount of the scholarship is not subject to penalty.

As with UGMA accounts, the funds in a 529 Plan are controlled by the account contributor. Unlike the UGMA accounts, the beneficiary of a 529 plan may be changed at any time. If one child does not attend college, the account may be used for another child or close relative.

There are no income limits on eligibility to contribute to a 529 Plan. However, the maximum amount permitted to be contributed varies by state. Generally, the amount is equal to 5 years of college expenses with most limits ranging from $100,000–$160,000.

Lawmakers have talked about exempting 529 plans from federal income taxes. However, nothing has been negotiated as of this writing. If you are debating between opening a UGMA or a 529 plan, you should check with your financial advisor. Both plans have advantages. With 529 plans, parents do not have to surrender control of the account when the child becomes an adult as with a UGMA. Also, the earnings get to accrue free of taxation until used for college. This sounds great but in some cases a UGMA may be a better alternative. Why? With a 529 plan, you don't pay taxes until the money is withdrawn. All gains are then taxed at the student's tax rate. Conversely, with a UGMA, you will be responsible for taxes each year. However, until your child turns 14, the first $750 in annual gains is tax-free and the next $750 taxed at the child's rate. Everything above $1,500 is taxed at the parents' rate. Once the child reaches 14, all gains are taxed at the child's rate. This means that some of the gains in a UGMA will be tax-free each year. Secondly, capital gains are taxed at the lower capital gains tax rate, as opposed to being taxed as income. Gains from 529 withdrawals are taxed as income to the student when received.

Prepaid Tuition Plans

Some states offer sponsored college savings plans that lock-in tuition rates at a predetermined price. These plans can be set up on behalf on any child. The child can be a relative or family friend.

In a prepaid tuition plan the money you invest is managed by the plan. You have no control over how the money is invested. You may typically purchase four years of undergraduate tuition and in some cases, room and board credits.

The investment gains are taxed as ordinary income for the beneficiary when withdrawn for college. Again, check with your advisor before participating in a prepaid plan. You must calculate the net after-tax value of this type of investment vehicle against opening a UGMA account. Additionally, depending on what investment returns the plan is guaranteeing, a UGMA may provide more dollars come college time then the prepaid plan is worth. Again, it is wise to speak with an expert.

Dennis P. Barba Jr.

Tools that make the difference

The following are tools that can make or break your financial future. They take a lot of planning and help from your professional service providers. No plan can be truly complete or effective without them.

– Estate Planning

– Asset Allocation

– Security Selection

Dennis P. Barba Jr.

CHAPTER FIVE:
Estate Planning

Estate Planning

An entire book can be written on the subject of estate planning and estate conservation. Without careful planning, the assets you spend a lifetime building can become significantly depleted by the time your heirs receive distributions. Only proper planning on your part can help ensure your assets are protected and that your wishes are carried out. Half-hearted efforts or bad advice may be worse than no action at all.

Many people assume they simply do not have enough assets to warrant an estate plan. They think it is for the rich and famous. However, even some of the most famous people have had their estates depleted due to improper planning. The following table illustrates several examples:

Name	Gross Estate	Net Estate	Percent Lost
Marilyn Monroe	$819,176	$370,426	55%
J.P. Morgan	$17,121,482	$5,227,791	69%
Elvis Presley	$10,165,434	$2,790,799	73%
John D. Rockefeller, Sr.	$26,905,182	$9,880,194	64%

Source: Dearborn Financial Publishing, Inc.

Estate planning deals with several key issues:

– Estate conservation and tax planning

– Management of your estate during your lifetime

– Distribution of your estate upon your death

You must be sure to deal with an expert in estate planning when drafting documents. Your attorney should be well versed in estate planning, as should any insurance professional you choose to use within the context of an estate plan.

Estate Conservation

There are several benefits of estate conservation including avoiding conflict, delays, and expenses connected with the settlement of your estate. The following are some additional benefits of estate conservation:

– Selection of heirs

– Selection of how and when heirs will receive your estate

– Selection of individuals or fiduciaries to manage estate

– Minimization of settlement costs

– Setting up guardianship for minor children

– Having liquid funds to cover funeral, settlement and tax costs

– Healthcare and financial decisions while incapacitated

– Avoidance of Probate

In certain instances, usually through the utilization of a trust vehicle, it is possible to avoid probate court. Why would one be concerned about probate? First, probate can be expensive. Depending upon the state, costs associated with probate can be as high as 8 percent of the estate's value.

Additionally, probate can be a lengthy process. Periods up to and exceeding one year are not uncommon in probate court. While the estate is tied up in probate, your heirs are left waiting.

Finally, probate is public. In most courts, probate proceedings are public records. Anyone could go to the courthouse and determine who are your beneficiaries, as well as who was owed money at your death.

Minimizing Estate Taxes

While there has been much talk of late regarding reducing or even repealing the "death tax" going forward, minimizing estate taxes remains a concern for many. Federal estate taxes can be as high as

55% for large estates. This does not include state taxes or settlement costs. There are some basic tools one can use within the framework of a basic estate plan. Be sure to consult with you estate planning attorney before deciding on any course of action.

Unlimited Marital Deduction. The unlimited marital deduction exempts all transfers of assets between spouses from federal estate and gift taxes. Thus, there are no estate taxes due when a husband or spouse dies and leaves their estate to the surviving spouse.

Unified Gift and Estate Tax Credit. Be sure to have assets split between spouses to take advantage of the unified credit provided by the government. Each spouse should have at least the unified credit in his or her name. For 2001 this number is $675,000. All to often, a couple will have a sizeable estate with the majority of assets titled in the husband's name. This does not take advantage of the unified credit.

Annual Gift Tax Exclusion. You are permitted to transfer up to $10,000 per person to any number of individuals free from federal estate and gift taxes. This means that you and you spouse could transfer up to $20,000 jointly each year to your children, grandchildren, nieces and nephews, or anyone else free from estate and gift taxes. This can be an excellent method of reducing your taxable estate over time.

Why not just have a will, or do nothing at all? What happens when someone has no estate planning and dies? This is called dying "intestate." These estates are placed in control of the probate court. The court will decide the distribution of your assets as well as guardianship of any minor children.

Many people are under the assumption that there are methods of property ownership that will avoid probate. However, there are many issues other than property ownership that will affect how your assets will be distributed.

Management of your estate during your lifetime

There are circumstances that warrant granting someone power of attorney during your lifetime. Granting someone power of attorney gives an individual the power and authority to act on your behalf in legal and financial matters. However, the typical power of attorney may not be applicable to a disability or incompetency. To be certain your affairs are handled by a trusted person in the event of a disability or incompetency, you will need additional agreements. When executing an estate plan, ask your lawyer about the following documents, and determine if they are necessary for your situation:

– Power of attorney

– Durable power of attorney

– Medical durable power of attorney

– Living will

Having the necessary paperwork in place can make a potentially difficult situation more manageable for your family.

Distribution of your estate upon your death

The aspect of estate planning most individuals focus on is how their estate will be distributed. We already discussed some potential pitfalls of probated estates. The most common method of estate distribution planning is through the creation of a trust. Trusts are a common technique used to control the distribution of estates. The use of a trust can minimize legal fees, probate fees, and income taxes. Some trusts can completely bypass probate.

What is a trust?

A trust is simply a legal arrangement under which one person or institution controls property given by another person for the benefit of a third party.

The person giving the property is referred to as the trustor. The person controlling the property is referred to as the trustee. Finally, the person for whom the trust benefits is referred to as the beneficiary.

It is possible and quite common for the same person to be the trustor, trustee, and beneficiary of their trust. Many people like the estate benefits of a trust, but do not want to give up control of their assets. Under a revocable living trust, this is fairly simple.

Let's examine the most common types of trusts used in estate planning:

- Testamentary Trusts
- Living Trusts
- A-B Trusts
- Irrevocable Trusts
- Life Insurance Trusts

Testamentary Trusts

A testamentary trust will enable you to control the distribution of your estate including naming of guardians for minor children and their assets. This type of trust is usually established by a will upon your death. With a testamentary trust, your assets will have to be probated.

Living Trusts

A living trust allows you to transfer title of your assets into a trust. These assets transfer from you as an individual to yourself as trustee of your trust. You may maintain complete control of your assets within a living trust. Also, living trusts are revocable. You can make changes to beneficiaries at any time. A properly funded living trust should completely avoid probate. This is one of the main benefits of a living trust. When you transfer your assets from your name into the trust, you technically no longer own any of the assets transferred. Therefore, there is nothing to probate when you die. However, your estate will still have to pay estate taxes.

A living trust offers additional benefits: First, Living trusts avoid having to be placed under a court-appointed conservator in the event of incapacitation or disability. Secondly, living trusts are private. Since your estate will not end up in probate court, your affairs will remain shielded from the public. Only interested parties to your trust agreement will have knowledge of your estate and it's distribution.

A-B Trusts

It is sometimes permissible to establish a single living trust with what's known as an A-B provision. Under this provision, when the first spouse dies, two separate trusts are created. The assets of the surviving spouse are transferred to the A trust and the assets of the deceased spouse are transferred to the B trust. This arrangement establishes two taxable estates which will be able to utilize the maximum exemption from estate taxes.

When the second spouse dies, the assets of both trusts then pass to the beneficiaries. As with a living trust, A-B trusts can completely avoid probate. In effect, an A-B trust can enable a couple to pass up to twice the exemption amount to beneficiaries free of federal estate taxes.

Irrevocable Trusts

If you are interested in minimizing estate taxes, you may have to give up control over some or all of your property. As with a living trust, your assets will be transferred into a trust. However, with an irrevocable trust, you give up control over the assets placed within this trust. It is quite difficult to modify this type of trust. Considerable attention and study should be completed prior to establishing an irrevocable trust.

Life Insurance Trust

If you are concerned about minimizing estate taxes, but do not wish to give up control over your assets, you may be able to accomplish this with an irrevocable life insurance trust. In a life insurance trust an insurance policy is placed in an irrevocable trust. This keeps the policy out of the your taxable estate and allows the proceeds to pass to your beneficiaries without federal estate taxes. You will not own the policy or be the beneficiary of the policy. You will appoint an independent trustee to pay premiums and distribute property at your death. Also, you will not own the policy. Your life insurance trust will both own and be the beneficiary of the life insurance policy. It is important to follow the rules regarding administration of an irrevocable life insurance trust. You should clearly review and follow all guidelines with your estate-planning attorney to avoid potential problems after your death.

It has become common to purchase a second to die life insurance policy within a life insurance trust. This type of policy insures the life of both husband and wife. The policy will pay the death benefit upon the death of the second spouse. The proceeds from this policy are typically used to pay estate taxes. Again, the trust will be the owner and beneficiary of the second to die policy. The trustee of the insurance trust will distribute the proceeds per your directions established upon the creation of the trust.

CLEAR THOUGHT #15

Be certain to fund any trusts established as a result of your estate planning. A trust that is not funded may deem your estate planning efforts null and void.

In summary, it is imperative that you and your family consult with a professional advisor regarding all aspects of your estate planning needs. It is never too early to address this important set of needs. Finally, estate planning is for everyone. Not just the ultra-wealthy.

CHAPTER SIX:
Security Selection

Dennis P. Barba Jr.

We want to focus this section on equity selection. Why? Because so many individual investors have bad luck when buying stocks. They increasingly buy high and sell low. What drives the decision for an individual to purchase a stock? This is a good question but a difficult one to answer.

Far too many times the reason for a purchase is impulsive or at the minimum, completed with little or no strategic initiative. The purchase is made because it is something to do, or because their broker or friend told them it is a good buy. How do you know the person recommending a stock knows anything about this company? Should you buy a stock recommended by a neighbor who appears to have a lot of money? Should you buy a stock because your stockbroker told you to? Should you buy a stock because it has dropped from 80 to 9 and it is now cheaper than it was last year? The answer to these questions is no. Time and time again, we buy stocks for the wrong reasons.

CLEAR THOUGHT #16

Stocks go down for a reason. This reason or reasons are usually not good.

How should you decide which stocks to buy? Building a portfolio and purchasing an individual stock is not that different from structuring a financial plan or businesses plan. There needs to be fundamental business reasons tied to every purchase. Additionally, there needs to be objectives set at the onset of each purchase. Why are you buying the stock, and under what circumstances will you not continue to hold the position? These two issues are rarely addressed before a purchase.

Many people have said it is much harder to know when to sell a stock then when to buy it. In my opinion, this is true. Anyone can decide to buy a stock for even the most impulsive reasons. However, they never quite know when to sell. If the stock falls, they do not want to admit they made a mistake, or do not want to realize a loss. Likewise, if the stock rises, they do not want to pay capital gains. The following are two scenarios I have witnessed hundreds of times during the past 15 years of managing money:

– An investor purchases a stock at $20.00 per share. There is some bad news announced from the company and the stock drops to 16. The investor is unwilling to take a loss, holds onto the stock, and in a year the stock is at 4.

CLEAR THOUGHT #17

When bad news is first announced, there is usually more to follow. Examine this first announcement of bad news and determine if the reasons you purchased the stock still hold true. If you never had good fundamental reasons for owning the stock, sell it.

– An investor purchases a stock at $20.00 per share. The stock steadily rises to $80.00 per share and then starts falling. The investor does not want to sell the position because he or she does not want to pay capital gains. One year later the stock is at $30.00 per share.

CLEAR THOUGHT #18

Hold a stock until it stops going up, or one of the key reasons you purchased the stock changes. When the stock stops going up and reverses, you must pay attention to the technical trading patterns of the issue. Take protective hedging measures or sell the position when a stock that has risen sharply suddenly reverses momentum.

CLEAR THOUGHT #19

Sell a stock when it's time to sell the stock. Do not let emotions or tax consequences dominate your thinking. It is better to sell a stock that has gone up 150% and pay the gains than to continue to hold the stock while it depreciates to a price less than what you originally paid.

CLEAR THOUGHT #20

"When you discover your are flogging a dead horse, dismount."

– Dakota Indians

Enough preaching. How does one develop a strategy for sound equity selection? Unfortunately, there is not a canned answer to this question. However, I can provide some general advice and share some of the techniques we have used over the years.

First, develop a methodology or deal with an advisor who has a methodology. This means you must have consistent reasons for making a purchase. You should know why you are buying the stock and what you expect from the purchase. Set objectives for when to exit the position on the upside as well as the downside. How is this completed? There are two methods of security analysis that have worked well for us over the years: **Fundamental analysis and technical analysis.** To bring true value to any investment decision, one must have a basic understanding of both schools of thought. Let's define each method of analysis:

Fundamental Analysis

Fundamental analysis is the study of economic, industry, and company-specific conditions in an effort to determine the value of a company's stock. Fundamental analysis typically focuses on key statistics within a company's financial statements to determine if the stock price is over or under valued.

There are several steps associated with fundamental analysis. The investor should analyze the current and future overall health of the economy as a whole, the industry sector involved, and the company in question.

For the purposes of this discussion, we will focus on the analysis of the firm itself. This analysis may include several factors that give the firm a competitive advantage. Such factors as management experience and competence, history of performance, accuracy of forecasting revenues and costs, growth potential, etc., must be examined. There is no right or wrong method of fundamental analysis. Again, it is important to have a systematic approach or discipline that is followed over time. I will share part of our philosophy used to select individual stocks.

The following are ten characteristics of a high-quality company that have been defined by Goldman Sachs, a well noted investment banking and asset management firm that we have found particularly useful in evaluating companies for purchase from a fundamental viewpoint:

1. A business that provides a high-quality product or service and has a sustainable competitive advantage.

Businesses that provide high-quality, value-added products or services, along with sustainable competitive advantages, will almost inevitably be a high-quality company. A sustainable competitive advantage is what differentiates a company from its competitors. This advantage includes such things as providing a superior product or service, having the leading market share, being the low-cost producer, possessing a superior distribution system, utilizing better information technology and computer networking, having superior research and development technology or offering the best customer service. Trademarks, trade names, and patents frequently provide the most compelling competitive advantages.

2. A superior management team that has demonstrated a desire to act in shareholders' interest.

A qualitative assessment of management is almost as important a determinate in deciding to buy a stock as is conviction about a business's fundamentals. Management should have a defined business objective and a strategy that it implements well. In the best companies, one or two closely related businesses typically generate 80% of revenues. Management must use assets and invest capital to generate superior levels of profit and growth. They must be innovative as well as able to anticipate and act on change. Management must demonstrate a desire to act in the shareholders' best interest.

3. Compound growth rate in Earnings Per Share (EPS) of 10%–12% over the last ten years.

The company should have reported a compound earnings growth rate of 10%–12% over the last ten years. To generate such a record, demand for the products or services must have been expanding. Continued demand must be present, as margin improvement is finite, and pricing flexibility is generally very limited.

4. Consistency in earnings growth.

The consistency of reported earnings demonstrates recurring demand on a predictable basis for a company's products or services. A company that exhibits this consistency will most likely have below-average vulnerability to a downturn in the economic cycle. High quality earnings from an accounting standpoint will better reflect the company's true earning power. More consistent, predictable, and higher quality earnings should merit a higher multiple.

5. Projected growth rate in earning power of at least 10% over three years.

Growth in earning power is always an important element in determining the value of a company. Thus, an investor should select companies with projected annual growth in earning power of at least 10% over three years. To achieve this expectation, demand for the products or services should meaningfully exceed the rate of general economic growth. In addition, the company should be the low-cost producer and have enough pricing flexibility to offset inflation. This rate of internal growth is important because it will provide an annual return and increase the intrinsic value of the company. In turn, the stock price, over the long-term, should reflect these factors. An investor should be willing to pay a greater multiple premium for a higher projected growth rate.

6. A strong balance sheet.

A company with a strong balance sheet should have the capacity to finance its growth. A company's operating income should provide a very secure level of interest coverage under varied economic conditions. A company's debt balance should typically not exceed 30% of its total capitalization. A solid balance sheet will help reduce volatility in reported earnings during a recession as well as reduce the risk of charges from write-downs.

7. A return on equity (ROE) that has averaged at least 19% for the last five years and is increasing.

A Company's return on equity (ROE) should have averaged at least 19% over the last five years and should be increasing. A high ROE enables a company to finance growth internally and to increase its dividend. A higher ROE Company can afford a higher payout than a lower-ROE company and still grow at the same rate. A company with a relatively high ROE and a favorable trend in profitability likely deserves a higher relative multiple.

8. The generation of free cash flow.

The best businesses tend to be relatively less capital intensive and generate significant free cash flow. A well-managed company that provides a high-quality, value added product or service and possesses a sustainable competitive advantage will be able to fund its required spending from operating cash flows and, hopefully, generate free cash. Such a business is also less likely to require high capital investment relative to assets. An investor must examine the capital spending needs, the investment in working capital required to finance sales growth, and the dividend payout. A superior management that has free cash flow can benefit shareholders in many ways, such as share repurchase.

9. International competitiveness.

Globally leading companies can increase unit volume through geographical expansion and improving market share. Several of these companies possess the managerial talent, superior research and development, distribution and marketing skills, and financial resources to generate relatively high growth rates in long-term earning power. Worldwide competitive considerations will frequently be more of a determinant of capital spending than the business cycle.

10. Reasonable purchase price.

Over the long term, the best way to earn high returns in the market is to own stocks of high-quality companies that are projected to grow at above-average rates and are purchased at attractive prices. This means that P/E ratios must be reasonable. Nevertheless, an investor should be willing to pay a few multiple point premium for a high-quality company.

It is when we discuss what is a reasonable purchase price that technical analysis should come into play.

Technical Analysis

Prior to beginning a study of technical analysis, it is important to understand the differences between technical analysis and fundamental analysis. **Technical analysis is the study of prices due to supply and demand. Fundamental analysis is the study of factors that have an influence on price changes.** A simple answer to an investor's question of "why did IBM go up yesterday" is "because there were more buyers than sellers". This may sound simple, but it's true.

CLEAR THOUGHT #21

Stocks go up because there are more buyers than sellers, and they go down because there are more sellers than buyers. Stock selection is simple supply and demand. As an investor you need to deal with someone who has a proven method to identify what makes the demand for a stock increase. Additionally, technical analysis must be used to confirm the fundamental opinion.

Like fundamental analysis, technical analysis is not an exact science. It's an art and takes considerable experience. Not all methods of technical analysis work the same for every stock. One method may give excellent buy and sell signals while another may not work for you at all. It's up to each individual to find a method of technical analysis that will fit his or her specific needs, and ads value to the investment process. You should deal with an investment professional who has a basic understanding of technical analysis. Furthermore, this professional should be able to define their methodology and practice of technical analysis within an investment decision.

Technical analysis topics begin with basic concepts and progress to more advanced topics, and include information on creating your own unique studies. The interpretation of market activity using technical analysis provides clues to the investor as to the future direction of price. Technical analysis will use a combination of price, volume and time-sensitive technical indicators to help determine the direction in price. This technical analysis can help confirm the fundamental opinion and assist in the decision of purchasing a stock at a reasonable price. We will briefly review two popular methods of technical analysis:

Relative Strength Ranking

Relative Strength Ranking (RSR) is based on the idea that most successful stocks must rank well as compared to the overall market based on several criteria. RSR measures the performance of a stock based on the past year's worth of data. Relative Strength Ranking is measured on a scale of 0 to 100, where each number can be considered a performance percentile out of all available individual stocks in the market.

Relative Strength Ranking can be used as part of an overall selection criterion for purchasing new stocks, and as verification for a stock that has limited potential for a major price advance. When using relative strength one should choose leading stocks with a high relative strength ranking and avoid lagging stocks with low relative strength rankings. Investors Business Daily has a useful section on Relative Strength Rankings.

Basic Charting

Again, a fundamental basis for technical analysis is that prices move due to supply and demand. If the demand exceeds the supply, the price will rise. If the supply exceeds the demand, the price will fall. Charts reflect this rise and fall. By studying this movement on a chart, you can predict future price trends.

The purpose of charting prices is to identify price trends as they begin to develop and to make purchase and sale decisions based on these trends. Another way of identifying price trends is by looking at past price movement. With each stock, trading patterns have been identified over the years and it is assumed that these patterns will continue into the future.

On a chart, prices are reflected in a series of highs and lows. The direction of these highs and lows make up the price trend. An *upward trend* would have a series of successively higher highs and lower lows. A *downward trend* would have a series of successively lower highs and lower lows.

CLEAR THOUGHT #22

When examining stock charts during technical analysis, seek stocks that have consistently achieved higher highs and lower lows.

When choosing a financial professional, be certain he or she has a working knowledge of technical analysis. Ask him or her to explain how technical analysis comes into play within their practice. Their firm should have a department, or at least a key individual whose sole practice is technical analysis. Technical analysis is a key determinate in the decision of buying a stock at a reasonable price. It is even more important in the decision to sell a position.

CHAPTER SEVEN:
Asset Allocation

Dennis P. Barba Jr.

There is substantial research indicating that *asset allocation* is more important to one's financial health than the selection of individual investment vehicles.

What exactly is asset allocation? Asset allocation is the process of building a diversified *investment portfolio* by combining various *financial assets* in appropriate proportions.

The asset allocation decision is one of the most important decisions you will make as an investor. You may think that security selection and market timing are the primary components driving a portfolio's performance, but these factors are only important when combined with a strategic asset allocation policy.

A *financial asset* is anything that produces income and can be purchased and sold. Stocks, bonds, and certificates of deposit (CDs) are all considered financial assets. *Asset classes* are groupings of assets with similar characteristics and properties.

CLEAR THOUGHT #23

Each asset class may perform differently in different market conditions. Therefore, careful consideration must be given to determine <u>which</u> assets you should hold and the <u>percentage</u> of your assets you should allocate to each asset class.

Efficient asset allocation takes advantage of the differences in performance of various asset classes. The relationship between the movements of asset classes is known as *correlation*. Asset classes with high correlations tend to move more closely together, meaning they tend to respond similarly to market fluctuations. Conversely, asset classes that have low correlations, for example, stocks and bonds, can reduce the volatility of the combined portfolio, because when one asset class is down, the other may be up.

CLEAR THOUGHT #24

To construct an efficient portfolio, asset classes with low correlations should be included. This should help reduce the portfolio's volatility, and potentially stabilize returns.

The ideal asset allocation mix will also take into consideration the investor's time horizon, liquidity needs, tax situation, investment expectations, and risk tolerance. Common sense tells us the more time you have to save, the more aggressive you can become. Moreover, the more risk you can accept, the more you can invest in equities, and the higher your returns can be over time.

Recent studies indicate that a portfolio's asset allocation is the dominate factor in determining its performance and, over a period of time, typically explains over 90% of the variation in the portfolio returns. Ibbotson Associates, an independent investment firm, ranks the importance of the three major determinants of portfolio performance as follows:

Asset allocation	**91.5%**
Security selection	**6.7%**
Market timing	**1.7%**

Asset allocation far exceeds the effects of both market timing and security selection.

Certain statistical terms can be used to help explain the conceptual basis of asset allocation.

The **mean rate of return** is the average return on your investment. In a case where a stock produces returns of 6%, 8%, 12%, and

14% over a four-year period, the mean rate of return is 10 percent annually (6+8+12+14 = 40/4 = 10). As in this example, the actual return in any given year may prove to be greater or less than the mean.

The spread of returns around the average is known as the **standard deviation.** The importance of standard deviation for your portfolio is that *it measures the variability of returns over time.* Standard deviation helps measure the risk associated with your investment. It is a statistical fact that 68 percent of the time, the return on your investment will fall between two figures on either side of the mean that correspond to one standard deviation.

In our example, if the stock has a mean return of 10 percent and a standard deviation of 2, then 68 percent of the time your return will lie somewhere between 8 and 12 percent.

The wider the spread of results you are prepared to accept, the more certain you can be in predicting them. So, in our example, if you go to the second standard deviation, you will find that 95 percent of the time your return will fall between 6 and 14 percent. When constructing an allocated portfolio, you should attempt to achieve the greatest possible returns with the lowest possible standard deviation.

The third statistical function is **correlation**. To improve your chances of achieving the average return annually, you need to diversify over a number of different investments with the same potential average return. If the prices of two asset classes always move together, so that when one moves up so does the other, they are said to have positive correlation. Conversely, if the prices of two asset classes always move in opposite directions, they have negative correlation.

If you can find two investments with perfect negative correlation, it is possible to eliminate risk while maintaining your average rate of return. This obviously is not easy to accomplish. However, risk can be mitigated substantially by utilizing correlation within an asset allocation strategy. Part of the value an experienced financial professional can provide, is to use the historical statistical information that is available on thousands of investments to build a diversified portfolio that is properly allocated to meet your objectives.

These statistical measures fall into *Modern Portfolio Theory.* Modern portfolio theory looks at the detailed historical behavior of different asset categories. In a given set of market conditions, some asset categories will outperform the market and others will underperform. This relates back to correlation. Modern portfolio theory uses statistical analysis to evaluate different combinations of categories to determine the best return for a given risk and time horizon. Of course, there are no guarantees, but the investor can see the statistically predicted range of performance of the portfolio in dollars. Additionally, uncertainty decreases as the time horizon increases. So, in addition to being a powerful investment tool, asset allocation can provide performance predictions useful in personal financial planning.

Many mutual fund groups now provide smaller investors access to asset allocation funds. Additionally, many brokerage firms now have powerful software that makes the asset allocation process easier.

Asset allocation is not a static activity. It is, in fact, quite dynamic. It is critical to measure your performance against your goals, and have regular consultations with your financial professional to discuss your situation and asset allocation strategy. As we have recently seen, fixating on a specific strategy can be detrimental to your portfolio.

If you choose to use asset allocation as an investment tool, and you should, there are four items you should review annually:

– Review your investment goals and adjust your allocation mix to reflect changes in your objectives.

– Rebalance your portfolio to maintain your desired allocation. Market performance will likely be altering your asset balances (in terms of dollar values in each asset class). When one asset class dramatically outperforms the others, the portfolio can become unbalanced. To take advantage of allocation, the portfolio should be rebalanced to adhere to the original asset allocation.

– Take a "big picture" look at performance and goals. Are you getting where you need to be? If not, you may need to make adjustments such as investing more, changing your risk level, or changing an objective. If you are ahead of your goals, you may have an opportunity to reduce risk.

– Take a look at the economy and outlook for various asset classes. If there is an obvious risk in your portfolio that can be mitigated by changing the asset allocation mix, act. Your financial representative should be able to assist you in this endeavor. For example, if you initiated an allocation strategy five years ago that included a 60% weighting in long-term fixed income securities, and it is clear that long-term interest rates will be rising, you may want to rebalance your allocation mix.

We've all heard stories of someone who bought a single stock at the right time and made a lot of money very quickly. But that's very rare. The "large position" strategy is for the *gambler*. Asset allocation is a prime and critical strategy for the investor.

CLEAR THOUGHT #25

Most gamblers will not succeed. Most savvy investors will.

CONCLUSION

Dennis P. Barba Jr.

The only thing certain about the future of your financial planning is change. Circumstances change, our lives change, markets change, and people change. Planning is the essential bridge between the present and the future that increases the likelihood of achieving your desired financial results. Planning is the cornerstone of effectively reaching your retirement objectives. Even though planning is considered the foundation of financial success, it is commonly the task most investors neglect most. Planning is essential for successfully achieving your financial goals. This is due in part to the fact that organizing your finances, motivating yourself to save, and controlling behavior towards reaching your objectives are dependent upon good planning.

Far too many of us depend upon ourselves to achieve financial independence. For most, this is simply not possible.

CLEAR THOUGHT #26
None of us is as smart as all of us.

Surround yourself with a team of qualified, experienced advisors to guide you towards a comfortable retirement. Pay attention to details. Getting and understanding the important facts is a key to good decision-making. Virtually all mistakes occur because we don't take the time, don't drive hard enough, or weren't smart enough to get the important facts. You can't get and understand all the facts. However, by surrounding yourself with the proper team, you have a better chance of winning the game.

CLEAR THOUGHT #27

Establish and maintain a calm sense of urgency.

It is better to do something, recognizing that it may not be the ultimate right thing, than to do nothing at all. Additionally, if you don't have a calm sense of urgency, the bottom will drop out of your planning efforts. Take the time to meet with the appropriate people and take the time to define, execute, and continuously refine your financial blueprint.

INDEX

Dennis P. Barba Jr.